Epitaph for An Auctioneer
& other epigrams

Tim Hopkins is a former teacher who has published two novels for teenagers, poetry for children and adults, in addition to articles for the educational press. He has also supplied jokes to cartoonists and television comedians. As a sideline he has written songs, a few of which have had some success, including one performed at Ronnie Scott's Jazz Club. ***Epitaph for An Auctioneer** & other epigrams is a collection of short verses*, now serious, now humorous.

Epitaph For An Auctioneer
& other epigrams

Tim Hopkins

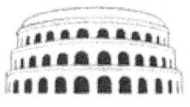

Arena Books

Copyright © Tim Hopkins, 2020

The right of Tim Hopkins to be identified as author of this book
has been asserted in accordance with the Copyright, Designs and
Patents Act 1988. All characters and events described in this book are
fictional and any resemblance to actual persons, living or dead, is
purely coincidental.

First published in 2020 by Arena Books

Arena Books
6 Southgate Green
Bury St. Edmunds
IP33 2BL

www.arenabooks.co.uk

**Distributed in America by Ingram International, One Ingram Blvd.,
P.O. Box 3006, La Vergne, TN 37086-1985, USA.**

All rights reserved. Except for the quotation of short passages for the
purposes of criticism and review, no part of this publication may be
reproduced, stored in a retrieval system, or transmitted, in any form or
by any means, electronic, mechanical, photocopying, recording or
otherwise, without the prior permission of the author or the publisher
acting as his agent.

Tim Hopkins
Epitaph For An Auctioneer *& other epigrams*

British Library cataloguing in Publication Data. A Catalogue record
for this book is available from the British Library.

ISBN-13   978-1-911593-66-9
BIC classifications:- DCF.

Cover design
by Anna Gatt

Typeset in
Times New Roman

CONTENTS

1
Epigram
2
Fiction
3
Paradoxical
4
Dust
5
The Nihilist
6
Writers & Critics
7
Critics
8
Concert-Goer
9
Plagiarist
10
Creative
11
Judge for Yourself
12
Mark My Words
13
Artless
14
Consolation
15
Inspired

16
Subjective
17
Seeing is Believing
18
Philosophical
19
Altruist
20
None so Blind
21
Shadows
22
Denial
23
Ambivalence
24
Diversity
25
Spectre
26
The Sophisticate
27
Chronology
28
Fresh
29
Sex in the City
30
Home Improvements
31
Fashioned Model

32
Plus Ça Change
33
Boat Rocking
34
Bedrock
35
Progress
36
No Exceptions
37
Captive
38
Bigot
39
Safety in numbers
40
Focus
41
Revealing
42
Greed
43
Dissonance
44
Rise and Fall
45
Face in the Crowd
46
Apparitions
47
Symbiosis

48
Expectations
49
Homage to Virtue
50
Strategy
51
Unknown Quantity
52
Heroic
53
Mannered
54
Self-Knowledge
55
Side
56
Insidious
57
Unfulfilled
58
Smug
59
Bigot
60
Surreptitious
61
In a Jam
62
Pharisaic
63
Ungracious

64
Doubtful
65
Not so Bright
66
Puffed-up
67
Not so Modest
68
Consequences
69
Wise
70
Self-Destructive
71
Sunshine and Rain
72
Reciprocity
73
The Life Unlived
74
Epitaph for a Centre-forward
75
Epitaph for an Auctioneer
76
Worth
77
No Closure
78
Eternal
79

79
Delayed Action

80
Epitaph

EPITAPH FOR AN AUCTIONEER

1
Epigram

A well-knit whole both pearl and plain
Whose fabric makes you think again.

2
Fiction

The elaborate lie
That cannot deceive
The cry of 'Wolf'
We can't disbelieve.

3
Paradoxical

Life is the truth
We cannot compute
Fiction, the lie
We cannot dispute.

4
Dust

Worthy volumes
By Authors long dead
The treasured canon
Of books unread.

5
The Nihilist

He believes in nothing and no one
But nonetheless wants to write
So he uses his pen like an inverse torch
Shining darkness into the light.

6
Writers and Critics

Those who can
Scribble
Those who can't
Quibble.

7
Critics

Like wasps these buzzing irritants
Are potentates of sting
And though their flight is like a bird's
Not one of them can sing.

8
Concert-Goer

He has no ear for music
But loves to drop a name
'My great-aunt knew Berg's cousin
And frankly that's why I came.'

9
Plagiarist

A parrot squawk
Of other birds
A canyon wall
Of others' words.

10
Creative

Work that's original
Rarely charms
It's welcomed with frowns
And folded arms.

11
Judge for Yourself

Bowdlerised work insults us
The body without the guts
If censors bleed as we do
Kindly show us the Cuts.

12
Mark my Words

Semi-colon is the pedant
Parenthesis the bore
Full stop the perfect house guest
Says enough but never more.

13
Artless

In underpass graffiti
We readily get the gist
Of a hundred grammar lessons
The scrawlers clearly missed.

14
Consolation

The artist freezes the moment
Stops turmoil in its tracks
And shapes it to the ordered peace
His own existence lacks.

15
Inspired

Godly or godless the artist
Is blessed like an unspoken prayer
Revealing with passion and wonder
A beauty that's already there.

16
Subjective

The world can be as various
As the pairs of eyes that see
And the moonlight shining through the trees
Has a billion ways to be.

17
Seeing is Believing

It is not the moonlit pine
Which evinces the divine
But the way we view it
The miracle is our reaction to it.

18
Philosophical?

Christian, Hindu, Atheist, Jew
When young believe what they're taught
And then as adults insist their views
Are the product of rational thought.

19
Altruist

Humanity he deeply loves
But people never please him
And as he cuts a global dash
His family never sees him.

20
None so Blind

Than a friend to all
None is more alone
Transparent to others
To himself unknown.

21
Shadows

Extroverts buoyant
Their spirits unsinking
Evoke in the doing
The thoughts they're not thinking.

Introverts musing
Involvement forsaken
Evoke in the thinking
The actions not taken.

22
Denial

Though women and men are different
By convention, this truth is abused
So weaknesses go unchallenged
And strengths are underused.

23
Ambivalence

A man who'd hoover, dust and clean
Of him she daily dreamt
Then married a dominant Alpha Male
From such demands exempt.

24
Diversity

Love is as various
As those who confess it
As sacred or sordid
As those who profess it.

25
Spectre

When courting a widow
There's a rival not seen
The ghost of a husband
Who walks between.

26
The Sophisticate

Text-book sex
Like being verbose
Is one more way
Of not getting close.

27
Chronology

He left his wife for his mistress
But their rôles might be reversed
Had the mistress he met second
Been the wife he married first.

28
Fresh

Forbidden fruit's
Exciting sap'll
Soon degrade
To mouldy apple.

29
Sex in the City

A fling with a wife in a neighbouring tower
Began as sweet as it ended sour
The moral of this for the urban strayer
The other side's concrete is always greyer.

30
Home Improvements

Who sharpen up partners
By changing them some
May take a dislike
To what they've become.

31
Fashioned Model

Slim-hipped, flat chested, skinny
She's the gay designers toy
Unwomaned by starvation
To the shape of his ideal boy.

32
Plus Ça Change

We can't be reborn to whatever we're not
(The lion was never an ass)
For genuine change is organic and slow
And never a showy volte-face.

33
Boat-Rocking

Conformist thinking
Fear no flak
Original thinking
Watch your back.

34
Bedrock

Blanket conventions
To which we assent
Are a patchwork quilt
Of past dissent.

35
Progress

Conman or benefactor
Nobody knows
But invite him in
He never goes.

36
No Exceptions

Justice for all
Or justice for none
The tyrant begins
By oppressing just one.

37
Captive

Who exploits others
With his own freedom pays
Linking fetters
Run both ways.

38
Bigot

A low bird
On a high perch
A narrow knave
In a broad church.

39
Safety in Numbers

We seek the distraction of others
In flight from ourselves and our fears
For solitude's deafening silence
Roars like thunder in timorous ears.

40
Focus

Friendship with a friend's friend
Totters precariously
Distinct prisms
We refract his light variously.

41
Revealing

Drink changes no one
It merely confides
The character weaknesses
Sobriety hides.

42
Greed

Garrulous men
Are gluttons' brothers
Consuming seconds
Apportioned to others.

43
Dissonance

The once successful slimmer
Gorges back to plumper state
Discomfited by slimness
Relaxed when overweight.

44
Rise and Fall

Fame achieved
Became a curse
Being forgotten
Was even worse.

45
Face in the Crowd

Honoured at last
An extra from TV
Appointed by the Queen
A.N. Other OBE.

46
Apparitions

Spectres trouble simple minds
At night with antics ghoulish
But never daytime scientists
No ghost would be that foolish.

47
Symbiosis

The hasty lender
Quick to defray
Begets the borrower
Slow to repay.

48
Expectations

From victims a villain wants virtue
Your attempts to deceive him he loathes
For although he may take your possessions
He won't have you stealing his clothes.

49
Homage to Virtue

From the annals of the honest
The robber takes a leaf
If you steal what he's just stolen
He gives chase and cries 'Stop thief!'

50
Strategy

Indifference thwarts the slanderer
For in stealing his powder and shot
We return his malice with interest
Our kettle immune to his pot.

51
Unknown Quantity

Happiness is the unpredictable guest
Who's at his worst when you demand his best
The more you stalk him the better he hides
The less you court him the longer he bides.

Happiness is the plan which goes awry
The X which pleases when you wanted Y
The wrong turning which becomes the right road
The last straw which completes the ideal load.

52
Heroic

An underrated bravery
Occurs when we desist
From injudicious escapades
The foolish can't resist.

53
Mannered

Excessive politeness
Like the poisoned chalice
Is artifice
Concealing malice.

54
Self-Knowledge

True to ourselves, the flatterer
Will waste each honeyed word
For knowing who and what we are
We see him as absurd.

55
Side

Those who show two faces
Have a third that's never seen
The face of authenticity
The person they might have been.

56
Insidious

Fair-weather friends are soon revealed
But worse are the parasite fools
Who feed on your sorrow and failures
And guzzle your life-blood like ghouls.

57
Unfulfilled

Poseur and fake
Resent success
True to ourselves
We envy less.

58
Smug

The conceited show no anger
And it's plain the reason why
As the rest of us are numskulls
Expectations aren't that high.

59
Bigot

A low bird
On a high perch
A narrow knave
In a broad church.

60
Surreptitious

The unpunctual are saboteurs
Whose apologies are fake
Their style is the slashed tyre
The loosened brake.

61
In a Jam

Our language when gridlocked
Is hardly seraphic
We're each of us drivers
But others are traffic.

62
Pharisaic

His public boasts of charity
Win favour at a price
Beneath the mask of virtue
Lurks the private face of vice.

63
Ungracious

Who boasts of acts of kindness
Is disesteemed no less
For vice slips in unnoticed
When virtue seeks to impress.

64
Doubtful

Who commends his talent
Is unsure of it
Who lacks honour
Speaks the more of it.

65
Not So Bright

Cleverness boasting its cleverness
Shows itself for a fool
For the ass who calls me a donkey
Will see me dig in like a mule.

66
Puffed-Up

Arrogance is never wrong
So cannot be corrected
Its hotline to reality
Forever disconnected.

67
Not So Modest

Who publicly turns down an honour
Pays the hypocrite's shabbiest price
For to boast of an honour's rejection
Amounts to accepting it twice.

68
Consequences

Everything the world has been
Informs the current way
No need to brood about the past
We live it every day.

69
Wise

Happy with who we are
This is the surest health
Happy with what we have
This is the surest wealth.

70
Self-Destructive

Set sights too high
Leave port in a gale
Contrive events
To ensure we fail.

71
Sunshine and Rain

Enjoying good fortune
Watch fate intervene
'You've bolted the good bits
Now eat up your greens!'

72
Reciprocity

Interdependence makes us brothers
Actions we take endure in others
None so rich and none so strong
Their lives aren't tempered by the throng.

73
The Live Unlived

The road we didn't travel
To the places never seen
Is the highway to IF ONLY
AND PERHAPS and MIGHT HAVE BEEN.

74
Epitaph for a Centre-Forward

Won penalties galore he did
By diving bless his socks
And now in death just as in life
He's flat out in the box.

75
Epitaph for an Auctioneer

God
Gave him the nod
And the bidding of the Lord
Cannot be ignored.

76
Worth

Decent people
By history underrated
Unobtrusive melodies
Sublimely understated.

77
No Closure

Life provides us every chance
To assess each chosen rôle
But death provides no retrospect
To view our lives as a whole.

78
Eternal

No consciousness before we're born
No consciousness when dead
Our mortal life is infinite
On Time's subjective thread.

79
Delayed Action

The stars' current light
Future nights will adorn
As a well lived life
Shines for those unborn.

80
Epitaph

True to the spirit
True to the letter
Made the world
One person better.

www.ingramcontent.com/pod-product-compliance
Lightning Source LLC
Chambersburg PA
CBHW020808160426
43192CB00006B/490